ON
LOVE

JOSEPH CAMPBELL ESSENTIALS

ON LOVE

JOSEPH CAMPBELL

JOSEPH CAMPBELL
FOUNDATION

New World Library
Novato, California

New World Library
14 Pamaron Way
Novato, California 94949

Text design by Tona Pearce Myers

Library of Congress Cataloging-in-Publication data is available.

First printing, January 2026
ISBN 978-1-955831-12-3
Printed in Canada

10   9   8   7   6   5   4   3   2   1

LOVE ITSELF is a pain, you might say—the pain of being truly alive.

THE TRUE MARRIAGE is the marriage that springs from the recognition of identity in the other, and the physical union is simply the sacrament in which that is confirmed. It doesn't start the other way around, with the physical interest that then becomes spiritualized. It starts from the spiritual impact of love—*amor*.

AS THOUGH STRUCK by lightning, so is one by love, which is a divine seizure, transmuting the life, erasing every interfering thought.

COMPASSION (German: *Mitleid*, "cosuffering"), unself-conscious love, transcends the divisive experience of opposites: *I* and *thou*, *good* and *evil*, *Christian* and *heathen*, *birth* and *death*.

LOVE WAS IN THE AIR in that century of the troubadours, shaping lives no less than tales; but the lives, specifically and only, of those of noble heart, whose courage in their knowledge of love announced the great theme that was in time to become the characteristic signal of our culture: the courage, namely, to affirm against tradition whatever knowledge stands confirmed in one's own controlled experience.

LIKE THE YIN/YANG symbol, you see. Here I am, and here she is, and here we are. Now when I have to make a sacrifice, I'm not sacrificing to her, I'm sacrificing to the relationship. Resentment against the other one is wrongly placed. Life is in the relationship, that's where your life now is. That's what a marriage is—whereas, in a love affair, you have two lives in a more or less successful relationship to each other for a certain length of time, as long as it seems agreeable.

SO WHEN PEOPLE think of marriage as a continuous long love affair, then they are bound for trouble. Because it isn't. It is in a proper sense an ordeal. And the ordeal is that of individual development. And if there isn't individual development taking place, well, what's the good of it?

AND I SAY if your marriage isn't the highest priority in your whole life, you're not married, that's all.

IT'S A VERY MYSTERIOUS thing, that electric thing that happens, and then the agony that can follow. The troubadours celebrate the agony of the love, the sickness the doctors cannot cure, the wounds that can be healed only by the weapon that delivered the wound.

THE PERFECT HUMAN being is uninteresting—the Buddha who leaves the world, you know. It is the imperfections of life that are lovable.

ANYTHING YOU DO involves a system of rules that state how a thing is to be done and done well. It has been said that art is the making of things well. And the conduct of a love affair—well, you could be a clumsy lout in this, but how much nicer to have the knowledge of certain rules that enable the expression to become more eloquent and gratifying.

LOVE IS the burning point of life, and since all life is sorrowful, so is love. The stronger the love, the more the pain.

ABSOLUTE LOVE is as dangerous to the efficient working of society as absolute hate.

THOUGHTS and definitions may annul one's own experiences even before they have been taken in: as, for instance, asking, "Can this that I feel be love?" "Is it allowed?" "Is it convenient?" Ultimately, of course, such questions may have to be asked, but the fact remains—alas!—that the moment they arise, spontaneity abates. Life defined is bound to the past, no longer pouring forward into future. And, predictably, anyone continually knitting his life into contexts of intention, import, and clarifications of meaning will in the end find that he has lost the sense of experiencing life.

IF YOU ARE SAYING "yea" to the world to improve it, please, just leave us alone. There is but one way to say yea in love, and that is to affirm what is there. That is true love.

THE MARRIAGE took place in the psyche first, and the physical realization of their love was the fulfillment of a spiritual marriage; it did not work the other way around. No priest confirmed the marriage. It was confirmed in love and was itself the sacrament of love. And neither lust nor fear, but courage and compassion, were its motivations, indifference to social opinion having been a prerequisite to its occurrence.

BEFORE [the troubadours], love was simply Eros, the god who excites you to sexual desire. This is not the experience of falling in love the way the troubadours understood it. *Eros* is much more impersonal than falling in love. You see, people didn't know about *amor*. *Amor* is something personal that the troubadours recognized. *Eros* and *agape* are *impersonal* loves.

IN THE MIDDLE AGES we find two principles of social life: living as one ought on the one hand; and on the other hand love, which ripped one out of this social norm.

IN THE RAPTURE of love one is transported beyond temporal laws and relationships, these pertaining only to the secondary world of apparent separateness and multiplicity.

LOVE THINE ENEMIES because they are the instruments of your destiny.

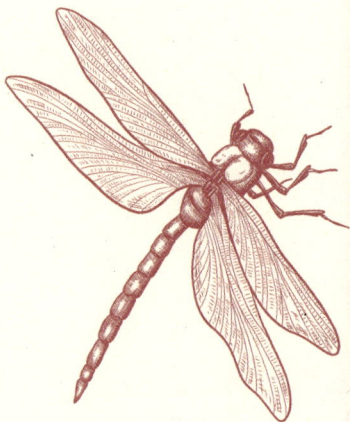

WE CAN NO LONGER speak of "outsiders." It once was possible for the ancients to say, "We are the chosen of God!" and to save all love and respect for themselves, projecting their malice "out there." That today is suicide. We have now to learn somehow to quench our hate and disdain through the operation of an actual love, not a mere verbalization, but an actual *experience* of compassionate love, and with that fructify, simultaneously, both our neighbor's life and our own.

IN GOTTFRIED [von Strassburg]'s world as well, the self-surpassing power of life, which is experienced in love when it wakes in the noble heart, brings pain to the entire system of fixed concepts, judgments, virtues, and ideals of the mortal being assaulted.

GOTTFRIED'S VERSION of the purity of love comprises thus two factors: a) uniqueness, singularity, unconditioned loyalty in the love experience, and b) a boundless readiness for the suffering of this love.

OUT OF LOYALTY to his love, in the midst of all this temptation, [Parzival] is not seduced. And in combat, he is never afraid. He is without fear and without desire—in the name of love.

ONE MIGHT SAY that the mighty jolt, which is the recognition of love, is nothing more or less than the sudden recognition that one is but a fraction, and that the completing fraction has been found.

NOW USUALLY when people talk of love, particularly in ecclesiastical circles, they contrast *agape* with *eros*, as though these two were the only possibilities. Both *agape* (spiritual love, Christian love) and *eros* (mere biological, physical love) are indiscriminate: *agape* ("love thy neighbor as thyself") means that no matter who your neighbor is you love that person, which is a fine sentiment of course; as for *eros*, it's really the lure and appeal of the organs to organs—in the dark anyone will do. In the early orgiastic cults, indiscriminate love was the rule; and one doesn't have to go back that far to encounter love of that kind. However, love as defined by the troubadours is different. Giraut de Bornelh, one of the great twelfth-century poets of Provençe, describes love as being born of the eyes and the heart—which is exactly what Dante said.

ONE HAS TO recognize that in domestic life there grows up a love relationship between the husband and wife even when they're put together in an arranged marriage. In other words, in arranged marriages of this kind, there is a lot of love. There's family love, a rich love life on that level. But you don't get this other thing, of the seizure that comes in recognizing your soul's counterpart in the other person.

HUMAN BEINGS are not perfect. What evokes our love—and I mean love, not lust—is the imperfection of the human being.

NOW COMES the great psychological thing. One falls in love at first sight. Now, what in heaven's name does that mean? You don't even know the person. Everybody, I hope, has had the experience. Somebody walks in the room, and your heart stops.

WHEN YOU HAVE two careers in the house and the individual developments are on two not always parallel courses, there's a lot of love required; I mean real pedagogical participation to help the other person to develop as a human being and still hang on to the relationship. The thing that holds them together is making the relationship the top thing. It's through the relationship that the development of each is taking place. And when you make a sacrifice, you are not sacrificing to the other person; you are sacrificing to the relationship. That relationship involves the progression of your own life.

MARRIAGE IS MARRIAGE, you know. Marriage is not a love affair. A love affair is a totally different thing. A marriage is a commitment to that which you are. That person is literally your other half. And you and the other are one. A love affair isn't that. That is a relationship for pleasure, and when it gets to be unpleasurable, it's off. But a marriage is a life commitment, and a life commitment means the prime concern of your life. If marriage is not the prime concern, you're not married.

THERE IS AN IMPORTANT idea in Nietzsche, of *amor fati*, the "love of your fate," which is in fact your life. As he says, if you say no to a single factor in your life, you have unraveled the whole thing.

FROM THE HEART [chakra]…this is when you bring that factor of love in. As long as the dishes aren't it, you're just trapped in the chore. When you love the dishes and you think about what they mean in your life, when they're your family's food, sustenance, and all, then it's all transformed into metaphor and you're free. And the whole idea of the Bodhisattva is, there is no difference in visual action, in what is seen in action, between bondage and release.

THE SIMPLE TASKS of our life, when you're doing them because they're a function or factor in the life that you love and have chosen and have given yourself, then they don't weigh you down.

TRISTAN WAS experiencing love—
Meister Eckhart was talking about it.
The pain of love is not the other kind
of pain, it is the pain of life. Where your
pain is, there is your life, you might say.

IN *AMOR*, the love wound—the sickness no doctors can cure—can be cured only by the one who issued the wound: namely, the one you fell in love with.

OF COURSE, Saint Paul says, "Love bereath all things," but you may not be equal to God. To expect too much compassion from yourself might be a little destructive of your own existence.

THESE BUDDHISTS are marvelous, with no complaints: This is world process, Buddha process.... This is real love. This is inexhaustible benevolence. This is the wisdom and virtue of the bodhisattva Avalokiteshvara and of Chuang Tzu. You get it from the Dalai Lama as well; he will never say a negative word. They read things positively. It's marvelous!

ANYONE FALLING in love will find that, while under the spell of this frenzy, the laws of hard fact are for him suspended. He becomes the creator of his own sweet world. They rightly say that Love is blind, love does not see the crude, ugly fact that everyone else beholds and which it has turned into a radiant delight. Moreover, if love presses on (or let it be anyone seized with a real passion), the laws that govern all prudent life will dissolve.

LOVE DOES not immunize the person to other relationships, let me just say that. But whether one could have a full-fledged love affair, I mean a real full-fledged love affair, and at the same time be loyal to the marriage— well, I don't think that could happen now.

IF A LIGHT BULB burns out and the superintendent of the building comes in and sees that it isn't working, he does not say: "What a pity! That is the bulb of all bulbs." He takes it out, throws it away, and puts in another bulb. What is important? Is it the illumination, or is it the bulb? What is important and of what are these bulbs the vehicles? They are the vehicles of light, or, for our purposes, of consciousness. With what do we identify ourselves, finally? With the bulb, or with the consciousness? The consciousness would not be there if the bulb were not there but it is the consciousness that is of significance here. When you have identified yourself with the consciousness, the body drops off. Nothing can happen to you. You are ready to be grateful to the body and to love it for having brought you to this realization, but it is only the vehicle.

THAT'S THE SENSE of courtly love in the Middle Ages. It is in direct contradiction to the way of the Church. The word *amor* spelled backwards is *Roma*, the Roman Catholic Church, which was justifying marriages that were simply political and social in their character. And so came this movement validating individual choice, what I call following your bliss.

IN DANTE also, the beginning of this journey, this personal call, comes into being through a distinctly personal experience of love, not through an undifferentiated experience. I have called this experience of personal love "aesthetic arrest."

FOR THE ABSOLUTE lover, as for the saint, the world with its values of honor, justice, loyalty, and prudence is well lost in the realization of desire. For the knight and lady of the world, however, such a mystic end of all in ecstasy is not, and never has been, the ideal of a noble life; and in twelfth- and thirteenth-century France it was not even approximately the courtly ideal of *amor.*

AGAPE is love thy neighbor as thyself—spiritual love. It doesn't matter who the neighbor is.

IF WE ARE DISTRACTED by certain sensuous interests, we'll marry the wrong person. By marrying the right person, we reconstruct the image of the incarnate God, and that's what marriage is.

THE RECOGNITION of the spiritual identity is what marriage is. It's different from a love affair. It has nothing to do with that. It's another mythological plane of experience. When people get married because they think it's a long-time love affair, they'll be divorced very soon, because all love affairs end in disappointment.

MARRIAGE IS not a simple love affair, it's an ordeal, and the ordeal is the sacrifice of ego to a relationship in which two have become one.

THIS ANGUISH was the great thing that the Middle Ages was interested in, the pain of love, which is the pain of life. Your life is where your pain is; you might put it that way. And it was the experience of the anguish that held the essence of life.

YOU MUST HAVE *amor fati*, the love of fate. And it takes an awful lot of guts to *really* say yes all the way.

THE MEETING with the goddess (who is incarnate in every woman) is the final test of the talent of the hero to win the boon of love (charity: *amor fati*), which is life itself enjoyed as the encasement of eternity.

HOWEVER, the great characteristic of Europe is recognition of personality, of the individual. There is no culture in the world with a tradition of portrait art comparable to that of the West—think of Rembrandt. There is a deep meaning in the individual. *Amor* has to do with *personal* love—the meeting of the eyes.

[HOW DOES ONE CHOOSE the right person?] Your heart tells you. It ought to. That's the mystery.... There's a flash that comes, and something in you knows that this is the one.

AND WHEN THE EYES have found an object that fascinates them, they recommend this object to the heart. If it is a "gentle heart"—that is to say, a heart capable not simply of lust, but of love—that heart is wakened, and love is born. This is specific. This is *amor*. It's not for everybody; it's for the gentle heart, whose scouts are the eyes.

AS IN THE POETRY of the troubadours, so in Gottfried's *Tristan*, love is born of the eyes, in the world of day, in a moment of aesthetic arrest, but opens within to a mystery of night. The point is first made in his version of the love tale of Tristan's parents, Blancheflor and Rivalin. For there was in their case no potion at work, inspiring magically a premonition a priori of the course along which they were to be drawn through sensuous allure, from love's meeting of the eyes, to love's pain, love's rapture, and on to death.

THERE WAS an essential requirement—that one must have a gentle heart, that is, a heart capable of love, not simply of lust. The woman would be testing to find whether the candidate for her love had a gentle heart, whether he was capable of love.

THE NAME OF THIS transformative center, *anahata* [the heart chakra], has the curious meaning "not hit," which is interpreted as signifying "the Sound that is not made by any two things striking together." For every sound heard by the physical ear is of things rubbing or striking together. That of the voice, for example, is of breath on the vocal cords. The one sound not so made is the great tone, or hum (*shabda*), of the creative energy (*maya, shakti*) of which things are the manifestations, or epiphanies. And the intuitive recognition of this creative tone within a phenomenal form is what opens the heart to love. What before had been an "it" becomes then a "thou," alive with the tone of creation.

THE UMBILICAL POINT, the humanity, the thing that makes you human and not supernatural and immortal—that's what's lovable. That is why some people have a very hard time loving God, because there's no imperfection there. You can be in awe, but that would not be real love. It's Christ on the cross that becomes lovable.

THE WOUND is the wound of my passion and the agony of my love for this creature. The only one who can heal me is the one who delivered the blow. That's a motif that appears in symbolic form in many medieval stories of the lance that delivers a wound. It is only when that lance can touch the wound again that the wound can be healed.

LIKE A FLOWER potential in its seed, the blossom of the realization of love is potential in every heart (or, at least, every noble heart) and requires only proper cultivation to be fostered to maturity.

IF YOU ARE going to describe a person as an artist, you must describe the person with ruthless objectivity. It is the imperfections that identify them. It is the imperfections that ask for our love.

AS TRANSCENDENT, according to [Giordano] Bruno's understanding, God is outside of and prior to the universe and unknowable by reason; but as immanent, he is the very spirit and nature of the universe, the image in which it is created, and knowable thus by sense, by reason, and by love, in gradual approximation. God is in all and in every part, and in him all opposites, including good and evil, coincide.

BUT THE MATTER of falling in love—someone walks in the room and that's it! Bang! You think: This is it, this is my life. This is something that occurs in many, many romances, not only in Europe but in Asia, as well. I've had that experience myself.

AND LOVE, not reason, is stronger than death. Love, not reason, gives gentle thoughts, and love and gentleness render form: form and civilization.

THIS DEATH to the logic and the emotional commitments of our chance moment in the world of space and time, this recognition of, and shift of our emphasis to, the universal life that throbs and celebrates its victory in the very kiss of our own annihilation, this *amor fati*, "love of fate," love of the fate that is inevitably death, constitutes the experience of the tragic art: therein the joy of it, the redeeming ecstasy.

ACCORDING TO this mysticism of sexual love, the ultimate experience of love is a realization that beneath the illusion of two-ness dwells identity: "each is both." This realization can expand into a discovery that beneath the multitudinous individualities of the whole surrounding universe—human, animal, vegetable, even mineral—dwells identity; whereupon the love experience becomes cosmic, and the beloved who first opened the vision is magnified as the mirror of creation.

I THINK THE PROBLEM today is that we're taught, or rather, we're given to think, that marriage is going to be a long love affair and that you're going to have a lot of fun with the *anima*. The fact is you're not having fun after the first ten minutes. You're in confrontation with a problem and it turns into an ordeal. The ordeal is of acquiescing.

THE PRINCIPLE of compassion is that which converts disillusionment into a participatory companionship....What you must render is compassion. This is the basic love, the charity, that turns a critic into a living human being who has something to give to—as well as to demand of—the world.

IT IS JUST this readiness to embrace love's pain along with its rapture that makes the noble heart exceptional.

THERE IS NO SUCH THING as a love that is either purely spiritual or merely sensual. Man is composed of body and spirit (if we still may use such terms) and is thus an essential mystery in himself; and the deepest heart of this mystery (in Gottfried's view) is the very point touched and wakened by—and in—the mystery of love, the sacramental purity of which has nothing whatsoever to do with a suspension or suppression of the sensuous and the senses, but includes and even rests upon the physical realization.

AS IN THE LOVE cult and songs of the troubadours, the loves of this world are always personal, specific.

MYTHOLOGY in a general way doesn't really deal with the problem of personal, individual love. One marries the one that one is allowed to marry, you know. If you belong to that clan, then you can marry that one but not that one, and so forth.

LOVE HAS nothing to do with social order. It is a higher spiritual experience than that of socially organized marriage.

TRUE LOVERS know instinctively that they are one; and they dwell, consequently, in that atmosphere of timeless delight which is the air of Paradise.

WHEREAS SOME MORALISTS may find it possible to make a distinction between two spheres and reigns—one of flesh, the other of the spirit, one of time, the other of eternity—wherever love arises such definitions vanish, and a sense of life awakens in which all such oppositions are at one.

THE "ESTABLISHMENT" may be understood as a system of laws through which one's experiences of life are filtered. One must be redeemed from this through the doctrine of love. From Christ's words, we have learned that we should love our neighbors. We are not—as in previous times—to hate our enemies, but to love them instead.

THROUGH OUR OWN experiences of the union of love we participate in the creative action of that ground of all being.

LOVE FOR LIFE includes a willing acquiescence in the pain of life for which the pain and agony themselves, and all that goes with them, are no refutation whatsoever.

AT THE VERY END of the *Divine Comedy*, Dante realizes that the love of God informs the whole universe down to the lowest pits of hell.

WITH RESPECT TO LIFE in the domestic sphere, marriages in the Middle Ages were marriages of convenience, made sacred by those clergymen in the sacrament of marriage. Love posed a danger to that.

AS I HAVE SAID, every one of these goddesses is the whole Goddess, and the others are inflections of her powers. Aphrodite is the divine goddess whose powers are inflected throughout the world as the power of love, of the dynamics of the energy represented by Eros, who is Aphrodite's child and a major deity of the classical pantheon—in Plato's *Symposium* he is the original god of the world. In her one aspect of lust she plays a role in the triad in which Hera also takes a role and Athena another, but she actually could play all the roles herself. As total Goddess, she is the energy that supports the *shakti* of the whole universe. In later systems,

the three Graces come to represent
three aspects of her power to send
energy into the world, draw energy
back to the source, and unite the two
powers.

THE IMPORTANT THING about information and the way that I got it is not the information but the *experience* of the information. It's a love affair, really, of getting in touch with a world of thinking and experiencing that you can't get from just the supplying of information.

THIS IS PUSHING right through the pair of opposites of life and death, and this is where love is: the pain pushed through.

SO WE SEE three—at least three— distinct periods of growth and susceptibility to imprint as inevitable in a human biography: (1) childhood and youth, with its uncouth charm; (2) maturity, with its competence and authority; and (3) wise old age, nursing its own death and gazing back, either with love or with rancor, at the fading world.

FALLING IN LOVE means losing
yourself in another object.

LOVE IS BORN of the eyes and heart: the light world of the godly gift of sight and the dark of the grotto that opens within to infinity. Hence, if the goddess Amor is to be served, neither light alone nor darkness can represent her way, which is mixed: neither Galahad's couch to Sarras nor the crystalline bed of Tristan's cave, but as long as life lasts—and life, after all, is her field—Gawain's Marvel Bed of bolts and darts ("Anyone seeking rest," states the author, "had better not come to *this* bed"), or the hard war-saddle of Parzival's turtle-dove-branded charger.

A THIRD SUGGESTION was offered by Saint Anselm's brilliant contemporary, the lover of Heloise, Abelard (1079–1142), but rejected by the churchmen as unacceptable; namely, that Christ's self-offering was addressed neither to the Devil nor to God, but to man, to prove God's love, to waken love in response, and thus to win man back to God. All that was asked for redemption was a response of love in return, and the power of love then itself would operate to effect the reunion that is mankind's proper end.

THE PASSAGE of the mythological hero may be over-ground, incidentally; fundamentally it is inward—into depths where obscure resistances are overcome, and long lost, forgotten powers are revivified, to be made available for the transfiguration of the world. This deed accomplished, life no longer suffers hopelessly under the terrible mutilations of ubiquitous disaster, battered by time, hideous throughout space; but with its horror visible still, its cries of anguish still tumultuous, it becomes penetrated by an all-suffusing, all-sustaining love, and a knowledge of its own unconquered power. Something of the light that

blazes invisible within the abysses of
its normally opaque materiality breaks
forth, with an increasing uproar.

THE SHRINE of the abbess Heloise was to a deity unrecognized by the offices of Abelard's theology: an actual experience, namely, of love, not for an abstraction but for a person; a flame of love in which lust and religion are equally consumed, so that, in fact, Abelard was her god. In her own words—and they may yet be crowned in Heaven as the noblest signature of her century—not the natural, animal urgencies of lust, not the supernatural, angelic desire to glow forever in the beatific vision, but the womanly, purely human experience of love for a specific living being, and the courage to burn for that love were to be the kingdom and the glory of a properly human life.

A NEIGHBORING KING, Clamide, sent an army under his seneschal, Kingrun, to appropriate [Condwiramurs's] land, when he would himself arrive and, in the good old way, make her his wife. "But I am ready," she says, "to kill myself before surrendering my body to Clamide. You have seen the towers of my palace. I would cast myself into the moat." This is the medieval marriage problem. The point is that she has resisted the system and demands to marry for love only.

IN THEIR CHARACTER as artists and in their poetry and song the troubadours stood apart.... The whole meaning of their stanzas lay in the celebration of a love the aim of which was neither marriage nor the dissolution of the world. Nor was it even carnal intercourse; nor, again—as among the Sufis—the enjoyment, by analogy, of the "wine" of a divine love and the quenching of the soul in God. The aim, rather, was life directly in the experience of love as a refining, sublimating, mystagogic force, of itself opening the pierced heart to the sad, sweet, bittersweet, poignant melody of being, through love's own anguish and love's joy.

THE WATERS of the fountains of inspiration dispensed to artists by the Muses, the liquor in the little pails of the guides and guardians of the mysteries, the drink of the gods, and the distillate of love are the same, in various strengths, to wit, ambrosia (Sanskrit, *amrita*, "immortality"), the potion of deathless life experienced here and now.

WHEREAS ACCORDING to the Gnostic-Manichaean view nature is corrupt and the lure of the senses to be repudiated, in the poetry of the troubadours, in the Tristan story, and in Gottfried's work above all, nature in its noblest moment—the realization of love—is an end and glory in itself; and the senses, ennobled and refined by courtesy and art, temperance, loyalty, and courage, are the guides to this realization.

SCHOPENHAUER, it will be recalled, treats of love as the great transforming power that converts the will to live into its opposite and reveals thereby a dimension of truth beyond the world dominion of King Death: beyond the boundaries of space and time and the turbulent ocean, within these bounds, of our life's conflicting centers of self-interest.

ONE CANNOT PREDICT the next mythology any more than one can predict tonight's dream; for a mythology is not an ideology. It is not something projected from the brain, but something experienced from the heart, from recognitions of identities behind or within the appearances of nature, perceiving with love a "thou" where there would have been otherwise only an "it."

IN THE TRISTAN ROMANCE, when the young couple has drunk their love potion and Isolde's nurse realizes what has happened, she goes to Tristan and says, "You have drunk your death." And Tristan says, "By my death, do you mean this pain of love?"—because that was one of the main points, that one should feel the sickness of love. There's no possible fulfillment in this world of that identity one is experiencing. Tristan says, "If by my death, you mean this agony of love, that is my life. If by my death, you mean the punishment that we are to suffer if discovered, I accept that. And if by my death, you mean eternal punishment in the fires of hell, I accept that, too." Now, that's big stuff.

WHAT IS DIFFICULT to leave, then, is not the womb but the phallus— unless, indeed, the life-weariness has already seized the heart, when it will be death that calls with the promise of bliss that formerly was the lure of love. Full circle, from the tomb of the womb to the womb of the tomb, we come: an ambiguous, enigmatical incursion into a world of solid matter that is soon to melt from us, like the substance of a dream. And, looking back at what had promised to be our own unique, unpredictable, and dangerous adventure, all we find in the end is such a series of standard metamorphoses

as men and women have undergone
in every quarter of the world, in all
recorded centuries, and under every
odd disguise of civilization.

SET APART from all spheres of historic change, the Venus Mountain with its crystalline bed has been entered by lovers through all ages, from every order of life. Its seat is in the heart of nature—nature without and within—which two are the same. And its virtue, so, is of the species, not of this particular culture, nor of that: Veda, Bible, or Koran; but of man pristine in the universe—which is something, however, that in this vale of tears is never to be seen, since we are each brought up (are we not?) in the ethnic sphere of this or that particular culture.

THE MYSTICAL THEME of the space age is this: the world, as we know it, is coming to an end. The world as the center of the universe, the world divided from the heavens, the world bound by horizons in which love is reserved for members of the in-group: that is the world that is passing away. Apocalypse does not point to a fiery Armageddon but to the fact that our ignorance and our complacency are coming to an end.

SOURCE TEXTS

The Ecstasy of Being: Mythology and Dance

Goddesses: Mysteries of the Feminine Divine

The Hero with a Thousand Faces

The Hero's Journey: Joseph Campbell on His Life and Work

The Inner Reaches of Outer Space: Metaphor as Myth and as Religion

The Masks of God, Volume 1: Primitive Mythology

The Masks of God, Volume 4: Creative Mythology

Myth and Meaning: Conversations on Mythology and Life

The Mythic Dimension: Selected Essays 1959–1987

Mythic Worlds, Modern Words: Joseph Campbell on the Art of James Joyce

Myths to Live By

Pathways to Bliss: Mythology and Personal Transformation

The Power of Myth

Romance of the Grail: The Magic and Mystery of Arthurian Myth

Thou Art That: Transforming Religious Metaphor

ABOUT JOSEPH CAMPBELL

Joseph Campbell (1904–1987) was a renowned American author and scholar of comparative mythology. His groundbreaking work *The Hero with a Thousand Faces* (1949) introduced the concept of the "hero's journey," a universal pattern found in myths across cultures. Campbell's theories were influenced by his studies in Europe, the work of Picasso and Joyce, Freud's and Jung's theories about the human psyche, his lifelong interest in Native American cultures, and his translation with Swami Nikhilananda of the Upanishads and *The Gospel of Sri Ramakrishna*. In 1988, the PBS series *The Power of Myth* brought his ideas to a global audience, solidifying his legacy in the study of mythology.

THE JOSEPH CAMPBELL FOUNDATION

(JCF) is a not-for-profit corporation that continues the work of Joseph Campbell, exploring the fields of mythology and comparative religion. The Foundation is guided by three principal goals: First, the Joseph Campbell Foundation preserves, protects, and perpetuates Campbell's pioneering work. Second, the Foundation promotes the study of mythology and comparative religion. Third, the Foundation helps individuals enrich their lives by experiencing the power of myth through community outreach and periodic Joseph Campbell–related events and activities.

JCF.org

John Bucher, Executive Director
Bradley Olson, Director of Publications